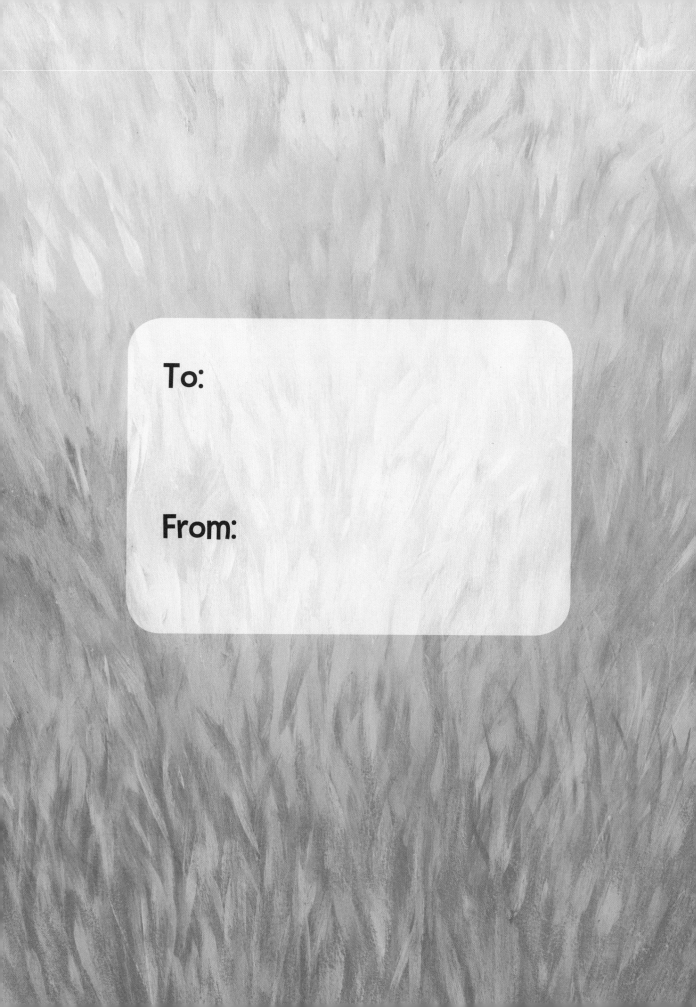

To:

From:

5-Minute Nighttime Bible Stories

© 2016 by Copenhagen Publishing House
www.copenhagenpublishing.com

Stories retold by Charlotte Thoroe
Illustrated by Gil Guile

Published in Nashville, Tennessee, by Tommy Nelson. Tommy Nelson is an imprint of Thomas Nelson. Thomas Nelson is a registered trademark of HarperCollins Christian Publishing, Inc.

Tommy Nelson titles may be purchased in bulk for educational, business, fund-raising, or sales promotional use. For information, please e-mail SpecialMarkets@ThomasNelson.com.

ISBN-13: 978-0-7180-8452-3

Library of Congress Control Number: 2015956560

Printed in China
21 22 23 24 25 DSC 12 11 10 9

5-Minute Nighttime
Bible Stories

The Old Testament

The New Testament

THE OLD TESTAMENT

THE BEGINNING

"Light.
I am going to make light,"

God said. Out of empty darkness,
God began the creation of the world
by putting light into the world.

God made everything from nothing.
He had the most wonderful plan for
everything He was going to make.

God spoke and whatever He said, it happened. God created the sky and the sea, the dry land and the plants.
God created the sun, the moon, and the stars.

How many different animals
are on these pages?

10

Then God started creating all the many
creatures living in the big oceans.

"Octopus! Shark! Jellyfish! Turtle!"

With every word God spoke,
He created another amazing animal.

Next, God made all the many animals jumping, running, and crawling on the earth.

"Hello, lion! Hello, little fox! Welcome, tiger! You are all perfect,"

God said.

On the sixth day God made a man. "Your name is Adam." God then made a woman. "Your name is Eve." God planted a beautiful garden called Eden for them to live in. "Take good care of everything I have made," God said.

On the seventh day God rested. He looked at all He had made and said, "This is very good."

Genesis 1–2

Dear God, thank You for creating such a beautiful world.

"Everything is good."

Noah's Ark

Time passed and one day when God looked at the world, He became very sad. Everyone had forgotten about God. People were doing bad things all the time. Then He thought about His friend Noah. Noah was a good man who listened to God.

God said to Noah, "I have a plan. I want to start all over again. A storm is coming, and a flood will wash away all evil. But you and your family will be safe."

Bonk-bonk-bonk!

God then told Noah that he had to build a big boat called an ark. It would keep them safe when the flood would come. So Noah built the ark.

How many animals are on these pages?

When the ark was ready, God told Noah to
gather together pairs of all kinds of animals.
Two by two, the animals entered the ark. Storm
clouds filled the sky. When Noah's family and all
the animals had climbed inside, the door was shut.

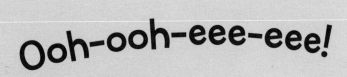

Ooh-ooh-eee-eee!

Drip, drop, drip, drop!

Then it started to rain. It rained for forty days and nights. First, water covered streets and houses. Finally, even the mountaintops were under water. But inside the ark, Noah's family and all the animals were safe.

Dear God, thank You for all of the wonderful animals and for always keeping Your promises.

Finally, the rain stopped, and one day the big ark came to rest on top of a mountain. God said, "Everybody can leave the ark now. The flooding is over. Send out all the animals." Noah opened the door, and all the animals rushed out into a fresh, new world. God set a rainbow in the sky. It was a sign of His promise to never again destroy the whole world with a flood.

Genesis 6–9

Boing! Boing!

The Tall Tower

A long time ago a group of people started to build a big city. Back then, everyone spoke the same language, so everybody in the whole world could say,

"Hello, how are you?"

and everyone understood. One day these people had an idea: "Let us build a really tall tower to reach up to heaven. Then we will always be remembered for what we have done."

How many people are working on the tower?

28

So they started building the tower, and it became higher and higher and reached up tall in the sky. The tower grew bigger, day by day, and people were getting more and more proud. "Look, see how tall and beautiful our tower is. We have made it with our own hands. We can surely do whatever we decide to do."

God knew what they were thinking.
He did not want people to trust in
only themselves instead of trusting in
Him. So God disrupted their plans. He
confused the people by giving them
different languages.

Now no one could understand anyone
else, and they could not complete
the tower. These people were instead
scattered all over the world.

Genesis 11

Bok-bok-bok!

Dear God, please help me to always put my complete trust in You.

Baby Moses in the Basket

There was an evil king in the land of Egypt. He was called the pharaoh. The pharaoh forced the Israelites to work as slaves for him to build his beautiful palaces and pyramids.

"There are too many Israelites,"

he said one day. So he ordered his people to throw all Israelite baby boys into the river.

Who is the baby in the basket?

Quack! Quack!

An Israelite mother had a little baby boy. The mother needed to hide her baby boy from the evil king and his soldiers. She hid him for three months, but then she could not hide him anymore. She and her daughter took the little boy, put him in a basket, and placed him among the bulrushes on the Nile River. Miriam, his sister, hid nearby.

Then an Egyptian princess came to bathe and found the baby in the basket. Miriam, who had been watching, asked the princess, "Would you like me to find someone who can take care of him?" The princess said yes and gave the baby to his sister.

"His name shall be Moses."

She also said, "I will pay all it will cost to raise this boy."

Exodus 1-2

Dear God, thank You for taking care of me even during tough times.

Da-da-da!

God Calls Moses

Moses grew up in Egypt, but when he was older, he ran away. He was angry that the pharaoh was keeping the Israelites as slaves.

One day Moses saw something very strange. A bush was on fire, but it was not burning away. Moses heard God's voice: "Moses, you must go and help My people. Go back to Egypt with your brother, Aaron. Tell the pharaoh to let My people go."

What did the staff turn into?

Hiss-hiss!

Moses went to the pharaoh and said, "Let the people go so they can have a feast for God in the desert." God also told Moses and Aaron to use a walking staff to prove to the pharaoh that He had sent them. Aaron threw the staff in front of the pharaoh. It turned into a snake. The pharaoh's magicians also turned their staffs into snakes.

"No, no, no! I will never let the people go. Never!"

shouted the pharaoh.

God then made ten terrible things called plagues happen in Egypt. Only the Israelites stayed safe. God showed His powers so the pharaoh would change his mind and set the Israelites free.

1. The Nile River turned into blood.
2. Frogs hopped everywhere.
3. Clouds of biting gnats filled the air.
4. Millions of flies flew everywhere.
5. All animals became ill.
6. Skin sores broke out on the Egyptians and on their animals.
7. Hailstones fell on crops.
8. Locusts ate all crops.
9. Darkness fell for three days and nights.

But the worst thing was yet to come . . .

10. The oldest child in every Egyptian family died.

Exodus 2–11

Dear God, thank You for taking care of Your people.

Neigh! Neigh!

God Makes a Way

After the plagues, the pharaoh agreed to let the Israelites go. He shouted, "Leave us alone! Moses, take your people with you and leave my country." Moses led the people out of Egypt. Soon after the Israelites left Egypt, the evil pharaoh regretted what he had done and wanted to bring them back again.

"Get my slaves back!"

he shouted and sent his soldiers after them.

When the Israelites left Egypt, they came to the Red Sea, but there was no way to cross it, and they had no boats to sail across it. Behind them the pharaoh's army came closer and closer. Everyone was very afraid. But Moses said,

"Don't be afraid. God will help us. We cannot do anything. But God will make a way."

What body of water did the Israelites need to cross?

"God will help us!"

Dear God, thank You for always helping me when I don't know what to do.

Then the most amazing thing happened. God sent a strong wind, and it blew the water of the Red Sea. The water moved to the left and moved to the right. God used the strong wind to part the waters, and a pathway opened up so that the Israelites could walk across on dry land. When the soldiers tried to follow, the waters rolled back and crashed down on them.

God's people were safe.

Exodus 12-14

Blurp-blurp-blurp!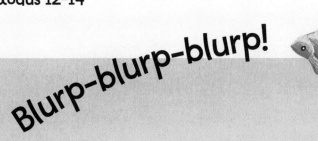

The Ten Commandments

Moses and the Israelites walked in the desert. They were hungry and thirsty, and it was hot. They started to complain. Every day God reminded them about Him and how He would take care of them. Each morning pieces of sweet bread, called manna, were lying on the ground when they woke up. God also sent quails into the camp that the Israelites could eat.

yip-yip-yip!

Splash!

How did the water come out of the rock?

One day they came to a place where there was no water at all to drink. The people started to complain again to Moses.

"Give us something to drink."

God told Moses to hit a rock with his stick and water would come out of it. Now the people could drink as much water as they wanted. But the people continued to complain and still did not trust in God.

God told Moses to go up on a mountain and speak with Him. God gave Moses ten rules for good behavior. God used His finger to write the **Ten Commandments** on two big stones. They are:

1. Do not worship any other god.
2. Do not worship a statue or a picture.
3. Do not use the Lord's name thoughtlessly.
4. Keep the seventh day as a rest day.
5. Respect your parents.
6. Never kill anyone.
7. Be faithful to your partner.
8. Do not steal.
9. Do not lie.
10. Do not want what other people have.

Exodus 16-17, 19-20

Dear God, thank You for the Ten Commandments so that we know how to make you happy.

Joshua and the Walls of Jericho

Joshua was a brave and strong young man. When Moses died, God said, "Joshua, you must lead the people to their new home, which I will give to them." They came to the city of Jericho. It had a high, mighty wall around it, and strong soldiers looked down from the walls. It was a fortress, and it stopped anyone from getting to the promised land. Joshua was not worried because God had already told him how Jericho could be defeated.

People asked,

"What now, Joshua?"

Joshua then ordered his soldiers and priests to march around Jericho for six days. The priests carried a gold chest called the Ark of the Covenant. Inside it were God's Ten Commandments He gave to Moses. On the seventh day the soldiers shouted and the priests blew their horns.

How many days did the Israelites march around Jericho?

"Pah-pa-rah," sounded the horns, and the big walls of Jericho came crumbling to the ground as if they were made of sand.

Finally, after all the years in the desert, the Israelites would reach the promised land.

Joshua 1 & 6

Crash!

Dear God, thank You for sending us strong leaders to follow.

Pah-pa-rah!

Whizz . . .

David and Goliath

David was a shepherd and helped his father take care of his sheep. As David watched the sheep, he learned how to protect the animals. He even fought a bear and a lion so he could keep the sheep safe. His brothers were soldiers in the army, and one day he brought them their lunches.

"Who dares to fight me?" shouted the giant Goliath. He was more than nine feet tall and carried heavy weapons.

"Ha, ha, ha!"

laughed Goliath because he knew nobody dared to fight him. He could see that all the soldiers in Israel's army were afraid of him. David's brothers, too, were very afraid.

What is the name of the Philistine giant?

"Don't be afraid!" David said.

"I will fight the giant!"

The king of Israel saw how David was not afraid like all his soldiers were. So he gave David his armor and weapons. But they were too heavy for David, and he took them off.

Plop!

David grabbed a stick.

One, two, three, four, five.

He picked up five smooth stones from a stream, and one of them he put in his pouch. Then he walked toward Goliath.

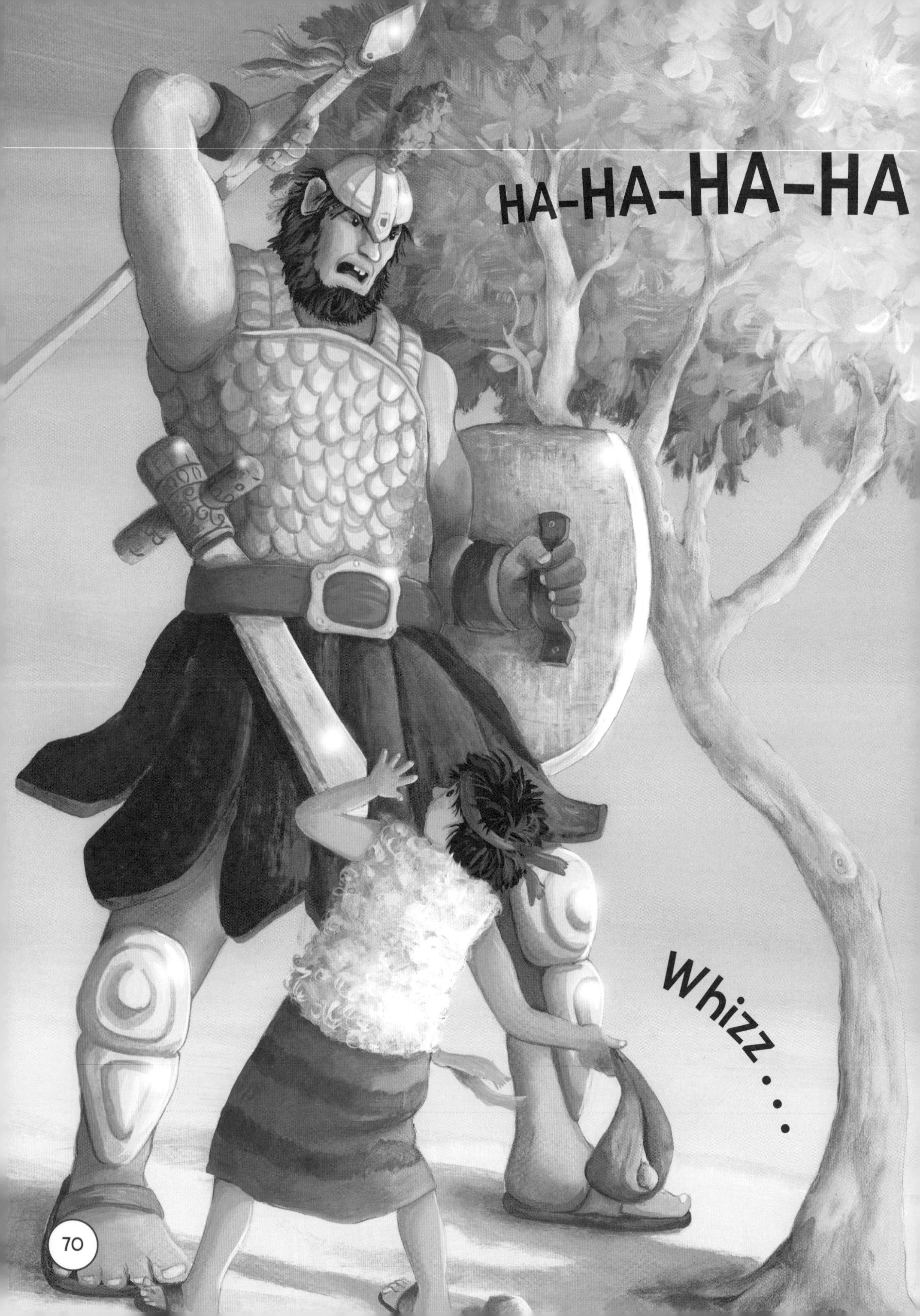
HA-HA-HA-HA
Whizz . . .

-HA-HA!

Goliath stood tall and strong looking toward David. "HA-HA-HA-HA-HA!" the giant shouted. "Do you think I am a dog? Is that why you have come after me with a little stick?"

David answered, "You depend on your own strength and weapons. But I trust in God, and I know that God will give me the victory!"

David then ran toward the giant while swinging his sling round and round. David sent off a stone, and it hit Goliath right between his eyes. Goliath fell facedown on the ground.

David defeated Goliath with a sling and a stone. When the Philistines saw what had happened to their hero, they started running away.

Crash!

The Israelites chased away the rest of the Philistines. David became a great hero.

1 Samuel 17

Dear God, please give me the strength to always stand up for You.

Daniel and the Lions' Den

Daniel worked for the king of Babylon. The king liked Daniel very much and said, "No one is working as hard and as well as Daniel. I want him to have the best job in my kingdom." This made the king's other servants very angry and jealous. So they decided to set a trap for Daniel.

Daniel loved God very much. So he prayed to God three times a day. Then the evil and jealous servants had an idea. They went to the king and said,

"We think there should be a new law. No one can pray to anyone other than the king."

The king liked the plan and made that new law.

How many times a day did Daniel pray?

But Daniel kept on praying to God. Daniel knew the men were watching him, but he was not afraid and knew it was more important to pray to God than to follow the new law the king had made. Daniel kept kneeling and praying to God every day. The servants knew their plan had worked.

The evil men went to the king and said, "Oh, great king! It seems that Daniel is praying to his God, not to you!" Now, the king was very sad because he liked Daniel. But he also knew he had to obey the law. So the king sent his soldiers to arrest Daniel.

The soldiers took Daniel, and as punishment, they threw him into a lions' den. "Roooaaarrr!" the lions roared. During the night, the king could not sleep. He tossed and turned and did not drink or eat anything as he thought about the lions and poor Daniel.

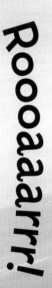

Roooaaarrr!

Early in the morning the king rushed to the lions' den and called, "Daniel! Are you there?" "Yes," Daniel said. "God sent an angel, and the lions did not harm me." The king was very happy and ordered Daniel to be pulled up from the den. Then he sent out a message to the whole kingdom of Babylon. It said, "Daniel's God is the best and the true God in the world.

Pray to Him instead—not to me."

Daniel 6

Dear God, thank You for protecting me.

Jonah
and the Big Fish

There was a man named Jonah.

God spoke to Jonah, "Go to the big city of
Nineveh. The people there are doing bad things. Tell them
to stop this. I will forgive them!" But Jonah did not obey
God. He went to the harbor instead and jumped on a
boat that was going to Tarshish, far away from Nineveh.

But it was not a good plan to try and run away from God. During the night, God sent a furious storm. "Help!" screamed all the sailors. "Oh no!" said Jonah. "This is my fault. I was not listening to what God told me to do! Throw me into the sea." The sailors looked at one another. Then they threw Jonah into the sea. **Splash!**

Oh no!

What kind of animal swallowed Jonah?

The men on the boat were safe. But poor Jonah was sinking deeper and deeper and deeper into the sea. God sent a big fish to rescue him. The fish swallowed Jonah with one big gulp.

Jonah slid all the way down into the belly of the fish. For three days and nights Jonah stayed inside the enormous creature. Sitting there in the darkness, he prayed to God. He asked God to forgive him.

God had not forgotten Jonah.

Then God made the fish spit up Jonah on dry land.

"Now I am ready to listen,"

said Jonah as he thanked God for helping him. God reminded Jonah about his job, and finally he went to Nineveh. Jonah warned the people in the city and told them what God had said. People listened to Jonah and asked God to forgive them. God forgave the people and did not destroy the city.

Jonah 1-3

Dear God, thank You for rescuing me no matter how far away I am from You.

THE NEW TESTAMENT

Jesus Is Born

Mary was a young woman. She lived in a small town called Nazareth more than 2,000 years ago. She loved God and had promised to marry a man named Joseph. He was a carpenter, and he, too, loved and obeyed God.

"Mary, do not be afraid."

One day God sent His angel named Gabriel to visit Mary. When Mary saw the tall and shining man standing there, she was very afraid. But Gabriel said, "Mary, do not be afraid. You are the most blessed woman. God wants to bring His Son into the world through you. You will become pregnant by the Holy Spirit, and you shall name the boy Jesus."

Whom did God send to Mary?

Even though it sounded strange, Mary trusted God and said,

"Whatever God says, I will do."

Joseph was very confused and did not know what to do when he learned about this. But God took care of everything. God sent His angel to tell Joseph to take Mary as his wife and also to be a father to Jesus.

Everthing happened just as the angel had said, and nine months later Mary was almost ready to have her baby.

At the same time, Mary and Joseph had to travel to Bethlehem by order of the ruler of the country. When they arrived in Bethlehem, every room was full. However, a kind man showed them a stable where they could stay. In the silent night Mary gave birth to Jesus.

God's Son had been born!

Matthew 1; Luke 1-2

Dear God, thank You for giving us the gift of Jesus.

"Don't be afraid!"

Visitors Arrive

That same night in the fields near Bethlehem, shepherds were watching over their sheep. Suddenly, there was a bright light in the sky, and angels filled the air around them. A shining angel said to them, "Do not be afraid. I bring you the greatest news the world has ever heard. God's own Son has been born this night in Bethlehem. You will find Him sleeping in a stable, wrapped in cloths and lying in a manger.

"Go now and worship Him!"

The shepherds hurried to town, found the stable, and entered. When they saw baby Jesus, they praised God and worshiped Jesus as their Savior. They knew in their hearts that this baby truly was the promised child and Savior of the world. The shepherds told Mary the angel's message, and Mary thought about all that had happened.

Moo! Moo!

How many animals are in the stable with baby Jesus?

Far away in another land, there lived some very wise men. They had been studying the stars, and one day they saw a bright new star in the sky. The star was the one that God had put in the sky when Jesus was born. They knew it was a sign that a baby King had been born. So they packed up their camels and followed the star.

"See the bright new star!"

Dear God, help me to worship You for all of my days.

The star led the wisemen to Bethlehem to the house where the family was living. When they entered and saw Jesus, they knelt down and worshiped Him. They knew He was the promised baby King they had been waiting their whole lives to see. They gave Jesus their fine gifts of gold, frankincense, and myrrh.

Jesus, the King of kings and the Savior of the whole world, had been born.

Luke 2 & Matthew 2

Jesus Begins His Work

We do not know much about what Jesus did when He was a young boy. But we do know that Jesus was trained to become a carpenter and that He learned these skills from His father, Joseph. The Bible also tells us that Jesus lived with His family and traveled with them to many places. Even when He was young, Jesus knew so much about God. When Jesus was thirty years old, He started speaking to people about God.

What skill did Jesus learn from His earthly father, Joseph?

Tweet! Tweet!

115

"Turn to God. Get ready. The kingdom of heaven will be here soon," shouted a man named John the Baptist. John was Jesus' cousin. One day Jesus went to see John as he was baptizing people in the Jordan River. Jesus went over and asked John to baptize Him. When He came up from the water, something amazing happened. A voice from heaven said,

"This is My Son. I love Him. I am very pleased with Him!"

The Holy Spirit came down from heaven upon Jesus like a dove. This showed that Jesus was ready to teach about God.

Matthew 3 & Mark 1

Dear God, help me to learn everything I can about You.

"Come and follow Me."

Come, Let's Go!

Jesus needed some helpers and friends to do His work on earth. He needed friends just like every person does. One day Jesus was walking by the Sea of Galilee when He saw some fishermen washing their nets. The men's names were Peter, Andrew, James, and John. Jesus called to them and said,

"Come and follow Me. I will teach you to fish for men instead."

Immediately the men left their boats and nets—everything they had—and followed Jesus.

Soon after Jesus met other men and asked them to follow Him. Jesus gathered twelve men. They wanted to follow Jesus and traveled with Him everywhere He went. Their hearts were full of joy over following Jesus and learning from Him. Meeting Jesus completely changed them forever.

Matthew 4 & Mark 3

Dear Lord, thank You for being a leader I will always seek to follow.

How many disciples did Jesus have?

Through the Roof to Jesus

In every town Jesus entered, He healed many people. The news spread that He was in Capernaum. A large crowd gathered to hear Him speak. Jesus was still teaching when four people came up, carrying their paralyzed friend on a mat. But they could not get their friend inside to Jesus because the house was full of people.

Woof!

The four men knew in their hearts that Jesus could heal their friend. They wanted to get him to Jesus. So the four men went to the roof above Jesus and made a hole in it. Then they lowered the mat with the crippled man on it.

How many friends helped the paralyzed man?

When Jesus saw how much faith these men had, He said to the paralyzed man, "My friend, your sins are forgiven." Some of the teachers of the law were there. They saw what Jesus did, and they said among themselves, "Why does this man say things like that? No one but God can forgive sins."

Jesus knew what they were thinking, and He said, "Why are you thinking such things? Do you not believe that I can forgive sins?" Jesus then said to the man,

"Get up! Pick up your mat and go home."

Immediately, the man jumped up, picked up his mat, and went out of the house while everyone praised God and said, "We have never seen anything like this!" Mark 2

"Praise God!"

Dear God, thank You for healing our bodies.

The Feeding of the 5,000

One day more than 5,000 people followed Jesus and the disciples to a place outside of town. It became late, and everyone was very hungry. "Jesus, send these people away now. Ask them to leave so they can go home and buy something to eat," the disciples said. Jesus said, "You give them something to eat." The disciples said,

"But, Jesus, we do not have any food, and we have no money to buy food for them."

"What food do you have? Go and see,"

Jesus said. Then the disciples found a little boy and took him to Jesus. He had brought two fish and five loaves of bread with him. Jesus said,

"This will do!"

So the little boy gave Jesus all the food he had.

Jesus said, "Ask the people to sit down on the grass." Jesus thanked God for the food and then He started breaking pieces off the bread and fish. He handed out pieces to the disciples and said,

"Give this to the people."

No matter how much they broke from the bread and fish, there was always something left.

How many fish and loaves did the boy give to Jesus?

Dear God, thank You for taking care of me especially when I can't take care of myself.

Soon everyone had eaten as much as they wanted. When everybody was full, the disciples gathered twelve baskets of leftovers. In Jesus' hands the little boy's five loaves of bread and two fish fed more than 5,000 people. It was truly a miracle, and Jesus was going to do many more miracles.

Matthew 14; Mark 6; John 6

Jesus Stops a Storm

One evening Jesus said to His disciples, "Come with Me across the lake." Jesus had been teaching and healing many people all day. So they left the crowd behind and went with Jesus in the boat He was already in.

There were also other boats that went with them. Jesus was very tired and fell asleep.

Suddenly, a very bad storm came up on the lake. The waves were coming over the sides and into the boat, and it was almost full of water. Jesus was still sleeping calmly. The disciples woke Him up and said, "Jesus, don't You care about us? We are going to drown!"

Why were the disciples afraid?

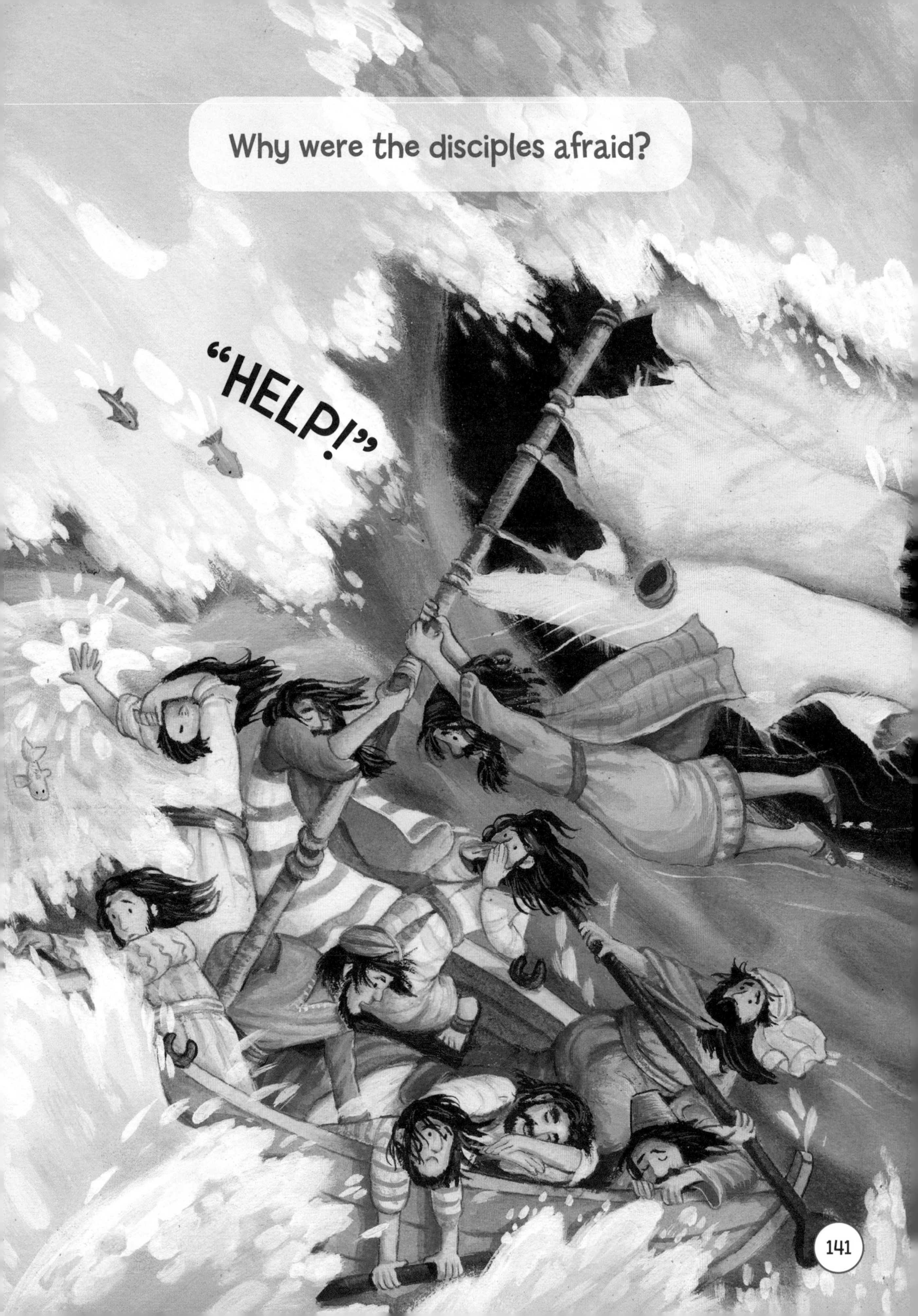

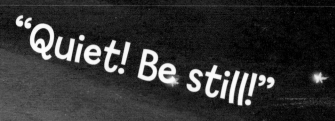

"Quiet! Be still!"

Jesus could see how afraid they were. He then stood up and shouted to the wind and the waters. He commanded, "Quiet! Be still!" Immediately, the wind stopped, and the lake became calm. The other boats were also safe.

Jesus asked His disciples, "Why were you afraid? Don't you have any faith in Me?" Now they were more amazed than ever. Even the wind and the waves obeyed Jesus.

Mark 4

Dear God, You are a mighty God who keeps me safe.

145

Birds and Flowers

People loved to hear what Jesus knew about God. Everybody loved to be near Him and listen to His words. People had never before heard anyone who knew this much about God's love. One day Jesus was teaching on the side of a mountain. Young and old people—they had all come to listen to Jesus, and they sat down on the ground around Him.

"Look at the birds," Jesus said.

What kind of people
came to listen to Jesus?

Dear God, thank You for thinking about me every day.

"Do they build barns and store their food? No! God feeds them every day. Look at these wildflowers. Where do they get their lovely clothes? Do they work every day to earn money to buy them? No! God dresses them in the most fantastic and beautiful colors. To God, you are so much more important than all the birds and all the flowers on earth.

God takes care of the flowers and the birds. He will also take care of you every day."

Matthew 6

Baaa! Baaa!

The Good Shepherd

Jesus loved to tell stories, and people loved to hear them because they always taught important things about God. Jesus told a story about a good shepherd. Jesus said, "Listen and try to imagine that you are a shepherd taking care of sheep. The good shepherd had one hundred sheep, and he took very good care of them."

"89, 90, 91, 92, 93,

94, 95, 96, 97, 98, 99 . . ."

"The shepherd knew every one of his sheep so well that he could tell if some of them were about to get ill. Every evening when they returned from the grazing fields, the shepherd would carefully count all his sheep before he locked them behind the fences. But one day he counted and realized that one little sheep was missing."

"Immediately, the shepherd knew he had to leave the ninety-nine sheep inside the fence and go find the missing sheep.

'There you are!'

shouted the shepherd when he finally saw the little sheep and rushed over to it. He took it, placed it on the back of his shoulders, and carried it back home. The shepherd was very happy because his sheep that had been lost was found and safe again."

Jesus then said, "This story was really about God. God is like the shepherd in the story, and every person who gets lost is like the sheep. God will, in the same way, look for and bring back anyone who has been away from Him. God's joy is so much bigger than the shepherd's.

Because people are so much more valuable to God than sheep are."

Luke 15

Dear God, thank You for watching over me just like a shepherd watches over his sheep.

Jesus Loves Children

Many people wanted Jesus to put His hands on their children and bless them. But Jesus' disciples tried to keep them away from Him. They thought that Jesus was too busy with more important things to do than talk to kids. "Jesus doesn't have time for small children," they said. But they were so wrong.

Jesus always had time for children.

What did Jesus say
about children?

"Don't ever send these little children away. Let them come to Me,"

Jesus said. "I can tell you this: If you are not going to be like these small children—full of trust in God in their hearts—then you will never understand what God is like. Be like these little children." Then Jesus put His hands on them and blessed them.

Luke 18 & Mark 10

161

Jesus Heals a Little Girl

There was a man named Jairus. He was very worried because his little daughter was sick and dying. Jairus had heard about Jesus healing the sick.

He rushed out of the house to get to Jesus.

Jairus bowed at Jesus' feet and begged Him,

"Please, Jesus, will You come to my house and make my sick daughter well again?"

When Jesus was on His way to Jairus's house, one of Jairus's servants came running and said, "I am sorry, master, but it is too late. Your daughter is dead." Jesus turned to Jairus and said,

"It is not too late. Trust Me!"

"Trust Me!"

Who was sick at Jairus's house?

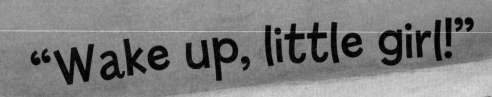

At Jairus's house everyone was crying. "The little girl is dead," they cried. But Jesus said,

"She is only sleeping."

People laughed. They knew for sure she was dead. Jesus then walked into the little girl's bedroom. He took her hand and said, "Wake up, little girl! It is time to get up!" The little girl opened her eyes and immediately stood up.

Jesus said to her parents, "Bring her something to eat." Jairus and his wife were completely surprised to see that Jesus had made their daughter alive again. Jesus had made them very, very happy parents. Their daughter was brought back to life because of Jesus' miracle.

Luke 8

Dear God, thank You for always having a plan for our lives.

169

Zacchaeus Meets Jesus

There was a man named Zacchaeus. He did not really have any friends because he took people's money unfairly. Zacchaeus was a tax collector. But he also took more money than he was supposed to, and he kept the extra for himself. So people did not like him at all. One day he heard that Jesus was in town, so he wanted to go and see Him. But because Zacchaeus was so short, he could not see above the crowd. He climbed up a sycamore tree so that he could see Jesus.

Why did Zacchaeus
climb a tree?

"Come down, Zacchaeus.
I will stay at your house,"
Jesus called.

173

Zacchaeus quickly came down from the tree. Zacchaeus was so happy to have Jesus in his house. But he knew he was a bad person who cheated people. Still, Jesus decided to visit him. Jesus had accepted him.

Zacchaeus said, "Lord Jesus, what I have done is wrong. Now I want to do the right thing. I am going to give half of my money to poor people. Next, I will pay back anyone I have cheated." Jesus smiled and said,

"Zacchaeus, I have come to save people just like you!"

Luke 19

175

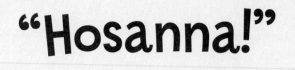

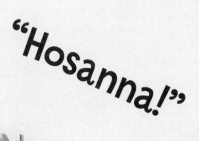

Entering Jerusalem

When Jesus knew God wanted Him to go, He traveled to Jerusalem with His disciples. He entered Jerusalem in triumph. Everybody was hoping He would be their new king and throw out the Roman soldiers. People shouted,

"Blessed is He who comes in the name of the Lord! Hosanna in the highest!"

But Jesus was not that kind of king.

While in Jerusalem, Jesus and the disciples gathered to share the Passover meal. This is called the Last Supper. Jesus shared wine and bread with them. He told the disciples to remember Him in this way when He was no longer with them. However, the disciples did not understand what was going to happen to Jesus. He knew it was nearly time for Him to leave the world and go back to God.

What is Jesus' last meal with His disciples called?

Dear God, help me to do what You want me to do, even when it's hard.

"Zzzzz!"

"Zzzzzzz!"

After the meal Jesus took the disciples to a garden called Gethsemane. Jesus asked them to stay awake and pray with Him. But they all fell asleep. Jesus was alone. But He needed to talk to His heavenly Father.

"Father, do what You want, not what I want,"

Jesus prayed. Suddenly, He heard loud voices and the sound of boots marching toward Him. It was soldiers who had been sent out by the leaders in Jerusalem. They wanted Jesus killed. The soldiers found Jesus, and then they arrested Him.

Matthew 21 & Mark 14

Jesus Dies

The soldiers took Jesus to the Roman governor Pilate who questioned Him. "So, are You a king?" Pilate asked. And Jesus calmly said, "Yes, but My kingdom is not of this world." Many people told lies about Jesus, and the crowd shouted,

"Crucify Jesus. We want Him dead!"

But it would be all right. This was God's plan. This was the reason Jesus was born into the world.

Why did Jesus have to die?

The next day the soldiers took Jesus to a place called Golgotha. They nailed Him to a cross. "Father, forgive them. They don't know what they are doing," Jesus said. Then there came a great darkness. Jesus said,

"Father, I give You My life! It is finished!"

Then Jesus died. He let Himself be punished for our sins. Some of His friends standing nearby were very sad as they went home.

"This is the end of Jesus," the leaders in Jerusalem said. Joseph of Arimathea asked for Jesus' dead body and laid Him in a new tomb where no one had been buried before. A big stone was rolled right in front of the entrance.

Mark 15; Luke 23; John 18-19

Dear God, thank You for sending
Your one and only Son to die for me.
"Arghh-arghh!"

Jesus
Is Alive Again

Early in the morning on the third day, two women both named Mary went to see the grave where Jesus was buried. But when they arrived, the soldiers were not there, and they saw that the big stone in front of the entrance had been rolled away. A man in shining clothes suddenly stood by them. The angel said,

"Don't be afraid. Jesus is no longer dead. He is alive again."

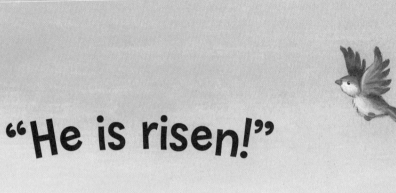

"He is risen!"

What did the women
find in the tomb?

Dear God, thank You for raising Jesus from the dead so that I can be with You one day in heaven.

After the other disciples saw the empty tomb and returned home, Mary turned around and saw a man. *Perhaps it is the gardener,* Mary thought. But really the man was Jesus.

Mary suddenly recognized it was Jesus when He said her name. She knew that He truly was alive again!

"Mary, go and tell the others that I am alive."

Mary was so full of joy. It was the most wonderful moment in her life. Jesus had been dead but now was alive. She could not wait to tell the news to Jesus' friends. Mary hurried to tell the others that she had seen the risen Lord.

Matthew 28 & John 20

Later Jesus also showed Himself to His friends, the disciples. They talked with Jesus and touched Him. They were no longer sad but full of joy. They now knew for sure Jesus was alive again. Jesus also showed Himself to many other people at many places and times. Jesus then said to His friends, "Don't be afraid of anything.

"Go now and tell everybody about how I have rescued every person in the world."

"Everyone who believes can come home to God and live forever with Him in heaven because of Me."

Not long after, Jesus' friends went to many places in the world and did exactly that.

Matthew 28; Luke 24; John 20

The Lord's Prayer

Our Father in heaven,
hallowed be Your name.
Your Kingdom come,
Your will be done
on earth as it is in heaven.
Give us today our daily bread.
Forgive us our sins
as we forgive those who sin against us.
Lead us not into temptation,
but deliver us from evil.
For the kingdom,
the power, and the glory are Yours
now and forever.

Amen.

Matthew 6 & Luke 11

THE TEN COMMANDMENTS

1. Do not worship any other god.

2. Do not worship a statue or a picture.

3. Do not use the Lord's name thoughtlessly.

4. Keep the seventh day as a rest day.

5. Respect your parents.

6. Never kill anyone.

7. Be faithful to your partner.

8. Do not steal.

9. Do not lie.

10. Do not want what other people have.

Exodus 20

David wrote many songs and poems praising the Lord. They are found in the book of Psalms. Psalm 23 tells of David's trust in the Lord. You can trust God too. God will take care of you. Just as He took care of David.

Psalm 23

The Lord is my shepherd.
I have everything I need.
²He gives me rest in green pastures.
He leads me to calm water.
³He gives me new strength.
For the good of his name,
he leads me on paths that are right.
⁴Even if I walk
through a very dark valley,
I will not be afraid
because you are with me.
Your rod and your shepherd's staff comfort me.
⁵You prepare a meal for me
in front of my enemies.
You pour oil of blessing on my head.
You give me more than I can hold.
⁶Surely your goodness and love
will be with me all my life.
And I will live in the house of the Lord forever.

Books of the Bible

Old Testament

Genesis	2 Chronicles	Daniel
Exodus	Ezra	Hosea
Leviticus	Nehemiah	Joel
Numbers	Esther	Amos
Deuteronomy	Job	Obadiah
Joshua	Psalms	Jonah
Judges	Proverbs	Micah
Ruth	Ecclesiastes	Nahum
1 Samuel	Song of Solomon	Habakkuk
2 Samuel		Zephaniah
1 Kings	Isaiah	Haggai
2 Kings	Jeremiah	Zechariah
1 Chronicles	Lamentations	Malachi
	Ezekiel	

New Testament

Matthew	Galatians	Hebrews
Mark	Ephesians	James
Luke	Philippians	1 Peter
John	Colossians	2 Peter
Acts	1 Thessalonians	1 John
Romans	2 Thessalonians	2 John
1 Corinthians	1 Timothy	3 John
2 Corinthians	2 Timothy	Jude
	Titus	Revelation
	Philemon	

Songs About Jesus

Jesus Loves Me

Jesus loves me! This I know,

For the Bible tells me so.

Little ones to Him belong;

They are weak, but He is strong.

Yes, Jesus loves me!

Yes, Jesus loves me!

Yes, Jesus loves me!

The Bible tells me so.

Words by Anna B. Warner